Crabapples

A Koala is not a Bear!

Hannelore Sotzek & Bobbie Kalman

🌲 Crabtree Publishing Company

Crabapples

created by Bobbie Kalman

For Peter and Chloe, with love

Editor-in-Chief
Bobbie Kalman

Writing team
Hannelore Sotzek
Bobbie Kalman

Managing editor
Lynda Hale

Editors
Niki Walker
Petrina Gentile
Greg Nickles

Computer design
Lynda Hale
Lucy DeFazio

Consultant
Michael Dee, Curator of
Mammals, Los Angeles Zoo

Illustrations
All illustrations by Barbara Bedell

Photographs
Animals Animals: Miriam Austerman: pages 18-19;
    Hans & Judy Beste: page 24; Patti Murray: pages 16-17;
    Fritz Prenzel: pages 30, 31
Erwin & Peggy Bauer: title page, pages 14, 15
John Cancalosi: page 25
Gerry Ellis/Ellis Nature Photography: cover, pages 4-5, 22
Photo Researchers, Inc.: Gregory Dimijian: page 19 (inset);
    Dan Levy: page 11
Tom Stack & Associates: John Cancalosi: page 28;
    Brian Parker: pages 8, 26-27; John Shaw: page 12;
    Inga Spence: pages 9, 20

Color separations and film
Dot 'n Line Image Inc.

Printer
Worzalla Publishing Company

Crabtree Publishing Company

350 Fifth Avenue
Suite 3308
New York
N.Y. 10118

360 York Road, RR 4,
Niagara-on-the-Lake,
Ontario, Canada
L0S 1J0

73 Lime Walk
Headington
Oxford OX3 7AD
United Kingdom

Cataloging in Publication Data
Sotzek, Hannelore, 1970-
    A koala is not a bear!

(Crabapples)
Includes index.

ISBN 0-86505-639-0 (library bound)   ISBN 0-86505-739-7 (pbk.)
This book examines the biology, behaviors, and habitats
of koalas, which are marsupial mammals.

1. Koala - Juvenile literature. I. Kalman, Bobbie. II. Title.
III. Series: Kalman, Bobbie. Crabapples.

QL737.M384S66 1997   j599.2'5   LC 97-5142
                                          CIP

What is in this book?

The koala

Koalas are **mammals.** Mammals are covered with fur or hair. Most baby mammals stay inside their mother's body until they are born. A mammal mother **nurses** her baby. She feeds it milk from her body.

Koalas are **marsupials**. A marsupial is a type of mammal. Most female marsupials have a pouch on their body. A marsupial baby lives inside its mother only for a short while. It is very small when it is born. The baby finishes growing in its mother's pouch or on her body.

The marsupial family

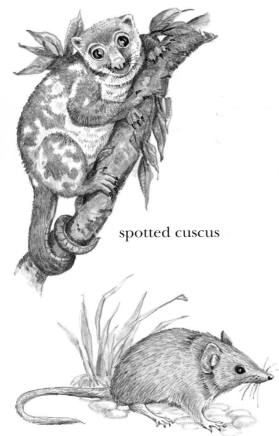

spotted cuscus

narrow-nosed planigale

common wombat

Koalas are part of the marsupial family.
Marsupials differ in size and shape.
One of the smallest is the
narrow-nosed planigale.
The red kangaroo is among
the largest and can be as tall
as a grown person. Some
marsupials, such as the
spotted cuscus, live in trees.
The cuscus holds onto
branches with its tail.
Another marsupial,
the common
wombat, is
a **burrower**.
Burrowers dig
holes and live
underground.

red kangaroo

6

There is only one koala species, but there are three **subspecies**, or types, of koalas—Victoria, New South Wales, and Queensland koalas.

Victoria koala
(southern koala)

New South
Wales koala
(southern koala)

Queensland koala
(northern koala)

Victoria koalas and New South Wales koalas are also known as southern koalas. Queensland koalas are northern koalas. The southern koalas are almost twice as big as the northern ones. Look at page 10 to see where these koalas live.

Not a bear!

Many people think koalas are bears
because they climb trees, have a thick
fur coat, and are chubby-looking.
Koalas are not bears! Both bears
and koalas are mammals, but only
the koala is a marsupial.

Bears have a layer of fat underneath
their skin to help keep their body
warm, but the koala has only its thick
fur coat to keep it warm.

Southern koalas have longer,
thicker, and darker fur because
they live in cooler temperatures
than the northern koalas.

Where do koalas live?

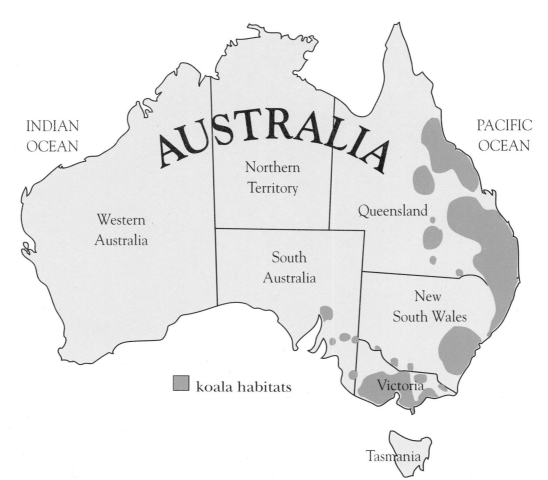

INDIAN
OCEAN

AUSTRALIA

Northern
Territory

Western
Australia

Queensland

PACIFIC
OCEAN

South
Australia

New
South Wales

☐ koala habitats

Victoria

Tasmania

Koalas live in forests along the east coast of Australia. Northern koalas live in Queensland. Southern koalas can be found in New South Wales, Victoria, and South Australia.

The koala is an **arboreal** animal. Arboreal means "living in trees." Koalas live, eat, and sleep in the top branches of eucalyptus trees, also known as gum trees.

A koala's body

The koala's body may look big and heavy, but it is well-suited to living high up in trees. The koala is very muscular. It uses its strong muscles to climb trees and hold onto branches.

A thick fur coat helps keep the koala warm when chilly breezes blow through the trees. The fur grows close together, keeping the skin dry.

The tail is small and stumpy, so it does not get in the way when the koala is resting on branches.

A koala's pouch opens to the rear. A special muscle controls the opening. When a mother tightens the muscle, the pouch closes. Her baby is kept safe inside the pouch and cannot fall out.

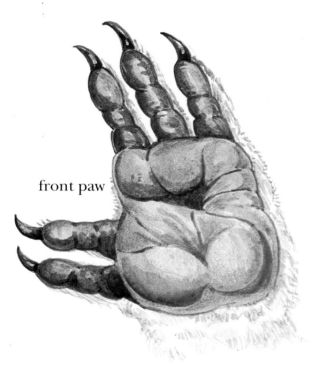

front paw

The koala has two "thumbs" on its front paws. They help grip branches. The sharp, curved claws on all four paws dig into branches.

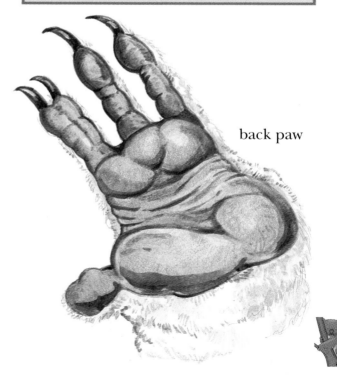

back paw

The toes on the back paws are spread far apart to wrap around boughs. Padding on the bottom of each paw stops the koala from slipping.

13

What do koalas eat?

Koalas are **herbivores**. A herbivore eats grasses, leaves, and fruit. Koalas eat mainly the leaves of eucalyptus trees, but they also eat cherry and tea tree leaves from time to time.

Sometimes koalas lick the ground. They may do this to get the salt and **minerals** their bodies need to stay healthy. Eucalyptus leaves do not contain salt or enough minerals.

Some eucalyptus trees have poison in their new leaves. The sensitive nose of the koala can smell which leaves are safe to eat. Only a koala can tell the difference between the safe and poisonous eucalyptus leaves.

In the trees

Living high in the trees helps protect koalas. The leaves hide them from eagles and owls that swoop down and prey on them. **Predators** that live on the ground, such as wild dogs, cannot reach the koalas. Trees also shelter koalas from rain and the hot sun.

The koala is one of the few arboreal marsupials that do not build a nest. When a koala sleeps, it holds onto a bough or wedges itself between branches so it will not fall.

Koalas are expert climbers. To climb, a koala reaches with its front paws and digs its claws into the bark of the tree trunk. It then pulls itself up by its front legs while hopping with its back legs. Sometimes koalas leap from branch to branch or even from tree to tree.

KOALA
CROSSING

On the ground

Koalas seldom leave the trees and go down to the ground. When they do, it is to move to a tree that is too far to reach by jumping.

A koala walks on all four legs. It is slow and awkward because its body is not suited to moving on the ground. When a koala is threatened by enemies such as dingoes, shown left, it can run short distances to a nearby tree.

Sometimes koalas have to cross a road to reach another tree. They must watch out for cars. Since koalas move mostly at night, it is difficult for drivers to see them.

Living alone

Koalas prefer to live alone. They are seldom friendly to one another. Sometimes more than one koala lives in a single tree, but each animal stays on its own branch. Mothers and babies are the only koalas that spend much time together.

Koalas make sounds and gestures to show how they feel. Even though they may look calm and cuddly, koalas can be noisy and nasty! Angry koalas often scratch or bite anyone or anything that bothers them.

When a koala is hurt or feels afraid, it lets out a wail that sounds like a crying baby. If you try touching a wild koala, it may scream. Male koalas sometimes make a bellowing sound to attract females.

21

Koala babies

A baby koala is called a **joey**. Most mother koalas give birth to only one joey at a time. Two joeys are difficult to care for high in the treetops.

When a koala is born, it is about the size of a kidney bean. It cannot see or hear and does not have fur. The baby's front legs are fully formed, but its back legs still need to grow. Using only its front legs and paws, the newborn koala pulls itself along its mother's fur and makes the long journey to her pouch.

Inside the pouch, the joey attaches itself to a nipple that provides it with nourishing milk. After six months, its mother's body makes a new food—a slimy liquid called **pap**.

Pap contains bits of eucalyptus leaves. The young koala licks the pap and learns to like the taste of eucalyptus. Its body gets used to digesting solid food.

About six months after the joey is born, its eyes open. It is now ready to see and explore the world outside. The joey leaves the pouch for a short time, but it hangs onto its mother's chest or back.

The pouch

The koala's pouch is useful for living in trees. It holds a baby koala, so the mother can use both hands for climbing. The pouch also allows a mother to take her baby along while she looks for food.

The joey uses the pouch as a safe place to rest when it is too tired to cling to its mother. The pouch hides a baby koala from animals that may want to eat it. It also keeps the joey warm when the weather is cool.

Koala facts

 Koalas are **nocturnal** animals. They are most active at night. During the day, koalas rest because it is too hot for them to move around.

Koalas drink very little water. In fact, "koala" is an Aboriginal word that means "no drink." Koalas get most of the water they need from the moisture in eucalyptus leaves, but sometimes they still need to drink.

The number of koalas living in one area depends on the number of eucalyptus trees that grow there. If there are more koalas than trees, some of the koalas find other areas where eucalyptus trees grow.

 Some people think koalas smell like cough drops because the oil from eucalyptus leaves is used in some types of cold medicine.

Most koalas have a **home range**, or a territory in which they live. Male koalas mark their home range by rubbing their chest against a tree trunk. Rubbing releases scented liquid from a gland on the koala's body. When a male smells the scent of another male on a tree, he knows to stay away from that koala's home range. Often, females and males live within the same home range. Females mark their territory with urine.

Koalas are strong swimmers, but they swim only when they find it absolutely necessary.

Koalas in danger

At one time, koalas were hunted for their thick fur, but now there are laws that protect them from hunters. Today, koalas face other dangers.

One of the greatest threats to koalas is the destruction of their **habitat**, or home. Many eucalyptus trees are cut down by people. Forests are cleared to make room for shopping malls, houses, and roads. Some trees are killed by diseases. Others are burnt in fires. When the eucalyptus trees disappear, the koalas that lived in them are left without a place to live.

The loss of eucalyptus trees threatens koalas with starvation as well as homelessness. Even when a koala must find a new area with eucalyptus trees in which to live, it may not eat the leaves of those trees. Most koalas eat only their favorite types of eucalyptus leaves.

Protecting koalas

People in special parks, called **reserves**, help protect koalas. Reserves provide the animals with food to eat and enough trees in which to live. Hospitals on reserves take in injured and sick koalas.

Some koalas are treated and returned to
the wild. Others are placed in zoos, so
more people can learn about them.
People can help save koalas and other
animals by not destroying the forests in
which they live.

Words to know

Aboriginal Describing something related to Aborigines, the native peoples of Australia

arboreal Describing an animal that lives in trees

gland A sac inside the body that produces a liquid

herbivore An animal that feeds only on plants

mammal A warm-blooded animal that has a backbone

marsupial A family of mammals whose females carry their babies in a pouch or on their body

minerals Crystals in the soil that are nourishing to plants and animals

nocturnal Describing an animal that is most active at night

pap A food produced by a mother koala that is a mixture of partly-digested eucalyptus leaves and dung

predator An animal that hunts other animals for food

prey An animal that is hunted by another animal for food

species A group of animals whose members share similar behavior or appearance

Index

3 4 5 6 7 8 9 0 Printed in USA 6 5 4 3 2 1 0 9 8